All Ab

Dana Carroll

Illustrated by Nicole Wong

Rigby®

A Harcourt Achieve Imprint

www.Rigby.com
1-800-531-5015

This is my house.

This is my room.

This is my family.

This is my pet.

This is my friend.

This is my school.

This is my teacher.

I LiKe Me!

This is my book!